Birds of the World

Meet Birds from Around the World

Rose Brown

Published by The Crackajack Company
Imprint: Brainy Bubs
ISBN: 978-81-69067-23-2
Text and concept by Rose Brown
This book is intended for educational and entertainment purposes only.
First Edition, 2026

Bald Eagle

United States of America

Did you know? Bald eagles can spot fish from miles away!

Peacock

India

Did you know? Peacocks fan their colorful tails to impress others!

Penguin

Antarctica

Did you know? Penguins can't fly but are amazing swimmers!

Flamingo

Africa

Did you know? Flamingos get their pink color from their food!

Toucan

Brazil

Did you know? Toucans have huge beaks but they're very light!

Ostrich

Africa

Did you know? Ostriches are the fastest running birds in the world!

Parrot

Australia

Did you know? Parrots can mimic human speech!

Hummingbird

United States of America

Did you know? Hummingbirds can hover in mid-air like helicopters!

Swan

Europe

Did you know? Swans mate for life!

Owl

Global

Did you know? Owls can turn their heads almost all the way around!

Kingfisher

India

Did you know? Kingfishers dive into water to catch fish!

Macaw

Brazil

Did you know? Macaws are among the most colorful birds in the world!

Kiwi

New Zealand

Did you know? Kiwis can't fly and have tiny wings!

Pelican

Australia

Did you know? Pelicans have huge beaks to scoop fish!

Sparrow

Global

Did you know? Sparrows are found almost everywhere in the world!

Canary

Spain

Did you know? Canaries are known for their beautiful singing!

Falcon

United Arab Emirates

Did you know? Falcons are one of the fastest animals on Earth!

Seagull

Coastal Regions

Did you know? Seagulls can drink both fresh and salty water!

Crane

Japan

Did you know? Cranes are symbols of peace and long life!

Robin

United Kingdom

Did you know? Robins are known for their bright red chests!

Albatross

Southern Ocean

Did you know? Albatrosses can fly for hours without flapping!

Cockatoo

Australia

Did you know? Cockatoos have crests they can raise on their heads!

Vulture

Africa

Did you know? Vultures help keep nature clean by eating leftovers!

Duck

China

Did you know? Ducks have waterproof feathers!

Puffin

Iceland

Did you know? Puffins are called “sea parrots” because of their colorful beaks!

Enjoyed this book?
Discover more fun and learning with other titles in the Brainy Bubs series by The Crackajack Company.
Each title has a companion storybook and coloring book.
We'd love your review.

9 788169 067232

Printed at Repro India Ltd.